The Erosion of the American Family

by

Gloria DiSanto

authorHOUSE®

AuthorHouse™
1663 Liberty Drive, Suite 200
Bloomington, IN 47403
www.authorhouse.com
Phone: 1-800-839-8640

First published by AuthorHouse 1/2/2009

ISBN: 978-1-4389-3205-7 (sc)
ISBN: 978-1-4389-3204-0 (hc)

Library of Congress Control Number: 2008910501

Printed in the United States of America
Bloomington, Indiana

This book is printed on acid-free paper.

Dedication

To my wonderful family thank you for all your support, especially for listening to all my ramblings through the years. Special thanks to my youngest son Fred for all his help and encouragement. And my son Anthony for all your editing & expertise.

Table of Contents

Dedication   v

Introduction   xi

Chapter One   Our Declining American Culture   1

Chapter Two   Judges in this Country   7

Chapter Three   Where is God?   17

Chapter Four   Our Kids   25

Chapter Five   The Media   35

Chapter Six   Politics   43

Chapter Seven   Race   49

Chapter Eight   Respect   55

Chapter Nine   Patriotism   61

Chapter Ten   Angelo's Pizzeria   65

Chapter Eleven   Drugs   75

Chapter Twelve   Illegals   79

Chapter Thirteen   What Can Be Done?   89

Epilogue   97

See what parents have done!

Parents are number one to blame!

Give, give, buy, buy; just do not bother to parent!

Entitlement is commonplace and parents are out of control!

Family values are not part of your home teaching and my question is why not?

Can it be that with the busy schedules you just do not have time?

Or perhaps you yourself were never really taught proper family values?

Let's examine all of this together

Introduction

As a grandparent, I have decided to take on the generation of my children. By taking them on I mean calling all parents of younger children and reviewing for them proper parenting skills. Everyday and all around, I watch error after error and have seen just how universal the parenting skills are today UNIVERSALLY INEPT. Was I a perfect parent? Of course not, is there such a person on this earth? I really do not think so! Parenting is a skill, a skill that none of you can ignore. It is a fulltime job that requires masterful thinking. Some of you get that concept. But unfortunately many of you do not. Now I ask you to read my thoughts and absolute facts and look deep into yourself. Maybe, just maybe together we can turn this epidemic of poor parenting around. My last book "Hit Them Harder" was to remind all parents that you can and should give that nasty child a smack when needed. Yes, parents you can punish your child! Forget the stupid "time out chair" that my friends, is a joke! You the parent are the keeper of those young beings; you are their role models. You are the molder of the clay that makes the whole person. Hold them dear to your hearts love them close. As

Theodore Roosevelt said "Walk softly, but carry a big stick" children love discipline, discipline goes hand in hand with love.

Giving is not the answer; sometimes you the parent think it is. After a few days with a new toy the joy diminishes. The new iPod becomes old and obsolete you already know that. And so it goes...

Each week something new and expensive is on the market. So time once again for you to buy. Wrong!

Technology is a wonderful thing, but are you aware that kids in high school do not know how to add or subtract without a calculator? This is a fact. E-mail, what a wonderful means of communication. However, most people never speak to their friends over the phone. Somehow this means of communication is so impersonal. Text messaging now the big thing! Kids are not even learning how to spell!

There is country western song out called "Don't blink" listen to the words. In all too short a time you child will be all grown up. Teach them to love, respect, and value patriotism. And all the ways to live a full life. Yes it is hard, but the rewards are worth it.

Chapter One
Our Declining American Culture

KIDS DON'T COME WITH INSTRUCTIONS.

PARENTS TODAY, IN MY VIEW, ARE LAZY.

PARENTS TODAY, IN MY VIEW, ARE SELFISH.

PARENTS TODAY, IN MY VIEW, ARE SELF- SERVING.

With that being said, what can be done to make our youngsters look into themselves and do basically the right things, yes you love your children. You want only the very best for that child. You just do not always know what the best is.

I wonder when it all changed, this child-rearing thing? Our culture has gone haywire! Look around you, what do you see? Look at Hollywood, there are so few decent people left in the move industry. Everyday we see and hear some appalling news about some actor gone haywire. Look at all the stars cohabitating. Marriage is a thing of the past. Look at all the stars having babies without begin married. Look at all the cheating stars, infidelity is commonplace. Look at all the drunk driving arrests. And we cannot overlook domestic abuse.

What is the message to our youths? Every magazine cover is some star doing something unacceptable. This list of bad behavior just goes on, and on it is really disgusting. Lets talk about people like Britney Spears, her stupid sister Jamie Lynne, Paris Hilton, Lindsey Lohan, and so many more, is this what we want in our daughters? I don't think so! Then we have men like Tom Cruise, who the hell is he? Sure, he too can bore a child without a marriage license. Again parents what is the message to our young people? These people are celebrated, why? Yesterday I heard that Brad Pitt and Angelina Jolie just gave birth to twins, who are they to flaunt their being unwed and having babies. We take this crap all in stride don't we? What have we become that all of this is…normal? What has become of the conservative?

Let us not forget some of the wonderful role models in Hollywood. Many great people who are married to the same people for many years. Nothing bad ever comes out about them, I could list many but most smart people know who they are. Years ago the academy awards were wonderful. We watched all the beautiful actresses and what they wore and saw all the great movies of our time win all the awards. Not anymore! Movies that win are about pregnant unwed teens, broken families, treacherous old men lusting after their daughter's girlfriends and homosexuality. I ask, what ever happened to the good old love stories? We all knew the couple was having sex but we never saw it. "It" (sex) was left to the imagination.

The newest attraction is actors using their celebrity for political purposes. They blast our president, they bash our military and we simply stand by and let it happen. But we can do something! I for one have made a conscious decision to not watch any movie where the star is negative about our country. I used to love some of the actors turned activist. No more, they will not get my dollar at the box office. They know we are a dumb bunch, so they just keep up their political rants. No matter what your political leanings are, Why do we celebrate them? Remember Barbara Streisand say she would leave the country if George W. Bush was elected? Guess what, she is still here. Duh!

The lowest form of Hollywood is Michael Moore. It makes me sick to even mention his name, his movie <u>Fahrenheit 911</u>. Americans actually went to see that movie. What are we thinking? What that movie did was demean our sitting President and our country. Only in America can you deface your country and make money doing so.

Again I ask: What message is this for our young people? Our country is headed for disaster. People like Moore and his kind will only bring this great country of ours down. The problems in this country have been brewing for years. If you think George W. Bush is the problem you are not well informed. Tell me folks, how can a mere actor change foreign policy?

So why do we condone people like Cindy Sheehan (who lost her son in Iraq) to expose her poison on the American people? We give her celebrity, why? Every talk show has her on to spew her hatred for America. What a telling commentary.

The actors who rant and rave anti American rhetoric are dividing our country. These people have the opportunity to unite our great county. Instead the dummies that believe are part of the division. Now coming soon we will have the opportunity to do it all over again. The 2008 election, lets vote them out!

I am talking about Hollywood; lets not forget to mention the music industry, gangster or "gansta rap." Our children buy these CD's. We as parents contribute to this trash. Just look at the money these so called "artists" are making. Millions! Bill O'Reilly took on these rappers not so long ago. He is the only one in the media who has gone after these so -called "artists"; the language is awful. I want you as parents to really listen to the words. They rap about their sisters, hos and all kinds of trash. Is this what your child is listening to? Be aware, and please take the time to listen.

Besides the music, what are we watching on TV? What are our kids watching? If it is MTV shame on you! Maybe you do not have the time to watch some of the videos. Please take the time.

To mention a few look at Eminem, his professional and personal life is a disgrace. Then we have Madonna, another disgrace. I could name so many more but I think you all know who they are.

Our teens are and have watched "Friends" a very popular show a couple years ago, I even enjoyed some of the shows. What was the message? Sleep with everyone? How about Two and a Half Men? Even the child in that series knows all about sex and the fact that his dad and uncle are sex machines. People actually love that show. This is incomprehensible to me that these shows are on primetime. I am sure you know all this but does it not bother you that your kids are watching it?

Chapter Two
Judges in this Country

Every day we hear of some outlandish ruling by a sitting judge. We have more bad people on the streets of our towns and cities because of our judges that make bad decisions. Yes we can change this. We must get savvy about our laws and we must research who is running for judges. I admit when I was much younger I would often just vote for a popular name or just re-elect an already sitting judge. Did I know anything about them? No, I did not. Not anymore though, our children's lives depend on good judges. We as parents should have our own personal judicial watch. Do we even know who our judges are? Why not? So many are way too liberal. Do not allow yourselves to believe the political adds on TV...INVESTIGATE! See how a certain judge voted, see how a judge has enforced the laws in your town. Be in the know. With the Internet today you can investigate these people. We need to understand, we the people run this country not bad judges!

Jessica's Law:

In 2004 Jessica Lunsford who was 8 years old was kidnapped, raped and killed in the state of Florida. Jessica's dad along with others started Jessica's Law. The law reads "any person who rapes a child automatically gets 25 years in prison." This law has spread to 44 states. Bill O'Reilly once again leads to have this law in every state. I believe that this law will be in every state before long.

We need to rid our communities of the aberration. Some people think treatment centers, support groups...etc, can help these people. That is simply untrue. The only way to stop this is to make punishment strong. Many judges are to quick to slap their wrists and send them back on the street. "11 years old is the average age of a child seeing porno on the Internet. Porno on the internet is a $57 billion dollar industry."

We, You and I together can get these bad liberal judges off the bench. We own the bench, judges work for us do they not? Let us protect our most precious assets our children. I pray that by the time this book is published all our states will have passed Jessica's Law.

We watch all the political ads. Some we believe, some we do not. As you watch in this very political time please know what is bull and what is the truth.

Don't we want our elected officials to be honest good people? Of course we do! RESEARCH! Do your homework before you vote. I voted for George W. Bush twice! I thought and still do to this day he is a good man. I hate war. Do I feel we should be at war? Yes I do. I think long after I am gone history will recognize what is right and why we need to be there. Do I think he made mistakes? Yes many. Out of control spending in Washington. Pork crammed in bills passed. If we were not in the Middle East now, I promise you we would be soon enough. It truly breaks my heart to see a story about a dead soldier. I pray with millions of Americans for our troops everyday. I honor those men and woman in the military. (You will read more in my political chapter coming up). This brings us to America vs. God. Did you know the Supreme Court opens every day with a prayer? Do any of us know the preamble of our state? Well now we will know. I have listed for you all the states preambles.

Alabama 1901, We the people of the State of Alabama, invoking the favor and guidance of Almighty God, do ordain and establish the following Constitution.

Alaska 1956, We, the people of Alaska, grateful to God and to those who founded our nation and pioneered this great land.

Arizona 1911, we, the people of the State of Arizona, grateful to Almighty God for our liberties, do ordain the Constitution...

Arkansas 1874, We, the people of the State of Arkansas, grateful to Almighty God for the privilege of choosing our own form of government...

California 1879, We, the People of the State of California, grateful to Almighty God for our freedom.

Colorado 1876, We, the people of Colorado, with profound reverence for the Supreme Ruler of Universe.

Connecticut 1818, The People of Connecticut, acknowledging with gratitude the good Providence of God in permitting them to enjoy.

Delaware 1897, Through Divine Goodness all men have, by nature, the rights of worshipping and serving their Creator according to the dictates of their consciences.

Florida 1885, We, the people of the State of Florida, grateful to Almighty God for our constitutional liberty, established this Constitution...

Georgia 1777, We, the people of Georgia, relying upon protection and guidance of Almighty God, do ordain and establish this Constitution...

Hawaii 1959, We, the people of Hawaii, Grateful for Divine Guidance…Establish this Constitution.

Idaho 1889, We, the people of the State of Idaho, grateful to Almighty God for our freedom, to secure its blessings.

Illinois 1870, We, the people of the State of Illinois, grateful to Almighty God for the civil I, political and religious liberty which He hath so long permitted us to enjoy and looking to Him for a blessing on our endeavors.

Indiana 1851, We, the People of the State of Indiana, grateful to Almighty God for the free exercise of the right to choose our form of government.

Iowa 1857, We, the people of the State of Iowa, grateful to the Supreme Being for the blessings hitherto enjoyed, and feeling our dependence on Him for a continuation of these blessings establish this Constitution.

Kansas 1859, We, the people of Kansas, grateful to Almighty God for our civil and religious privileges establish this Constitution.

Kentucky 1891, We, the people of the Commonwealth are grateful to Almighty God for the civil, political and religious liberties…

Louisiana 1921, We, the people of the State of Louisiana, grateful to Almighty God for the civil, political and religious liberties we enjoy.

Maine 1820, We the People of Maine acknowledging with grateful hearts the goodness of the Sovereign Ruler of the Universe in affording us an opportunity…And imploring His aid and direction.

Maryland 1776, We, the people of the state of Maryland, grateful to Almighty God for our civil and religious liberty…

Massachusetts 1780, We…the people of Massachusetts, acknowledging with grateful hearts, the goodness of the Great Legislator of the Universe. In the course of His Providences, and opportunity and devoutly imploring His direction…

Michigan 1908, We, the people of the State of Michigan, grateful to Almighty God for the blessings of freedom establish this Constitution.

Minnesota, 1857, We, the people of the State of Minnesota, grateful to God for our civil and religious liberty, and desiring to perpetuate its blessings

Mississippi 1890, We, the people of Mississippi in convention assembled, grateful to Almighty God, and invoking His blessing on our work.

Missouri 1845, We, the people of Missouri, with profound reverence for the Supreme Ruler of the Universe, and grateful for His goodness…Establish this Constitution.

Montana 1889, We, the people of Montana, grateful to Almighty God for the blessings of liberty establish this Constitution.

Nebraska 1875, We, the people, grateful to Almighty God for our freedom…Establish this Constitution.

Nevada 1864, We the people of the State of Nevada, grateful to Almighty God for our freedom establish this Constitution.

New Hampshire 1792, Part I. Art. I. Sec. V. Every individual has a natural and unalienable right to worship God according to the dictates of his own conscience.

New Jersey 1844, We, the people of the State of New Jersey, grateful to Almighty God for civil and religious liberty which He hath so long permitted us to enjoy, and looking to Him for a blessing on our endeavors.

New Mexico 1911, We, the people of New Mexico, grateful to Almighty God or the blessings of liberty.

New York 1846, We, the people of the State of New York, grateful to Almighty God for our freedom, in order to secure its blessings.

North Carolina 1868, We the people of the State of North Carolina, grateful to Almighty God, the Sovereign Ruler of Nations, for our civil, political, and religious liberties, and acknowledging our dependence upon Him for the continuance of those...

North Dakota 1889, We, the people of North Dakota, grateful to Almighty God for the blessings of civil and religious liberty, do ordain...

Ohio 1852, We the people of the state of Ohio, grateful to Almighty God for our freedom, to secure its blessings and to promote our common.

Oklahoma 1907, Invoking the guidance of Almighty God, in order to secure and perpetuate the blessings of liberty...establish this.

Oregon 1857, Bill of Rights, Article I. Section 2 All the men shall be secure in the Natural right, to worship Almighty God according to the dictates of their consciences..

Pennsylvania 1776, We, the people of Pennsylvania, grateful to Almighty God for the blessings of civil and religious liberty, and humbly invoking His guidance.

Rhode Island 1842, We the people of the State of Rhode Island grateful to Almighty God for the civil and religious liberty which He hath so long permitted us to enjoy, and looking to Him for a blessing.

South Carolina 1778, We, the people of the State of South Carolina grateful to God for our liberties, do ordain and establish the Constitution.

South Dakota 1889, We, the people of South Dakota, grateful to Almighty God for our civil and religious liberties.

Tennessee 1796, Art. XI.III. That all men have a natural and indefeasible right to worship Almighty God according to the dictates of their conscience…

Texas 1845, We the People of the Republic of Texas, acknowledging, with gratitude, the grace and beneficence of God.

Utah 1896, Grateful to Almighty God for life and liberty, we establish this Constitution.

Vermont 1777, Whereas all government ought to enable the individuals who compose it to enjoy their natural rights, and other blessings which the Author of Existence has bestowed on man.

Virginia 1776, Bill of Rights, XVI Religion, or the Duty which we owe our Creator can be directed only by Reason and that it is the mutual duty of all to practice Christian Forbearance, Love and Charity towards each other.

Washington 1889, We the People of the State of Washington, grateful tot the Supreme Ruler of the Universe for our liberties, do ordain the Constitution.

West Virginia 1872, Since through Divine Providence we enjoy the blessings of civil, political and religious liberty, we, the people of West Virginia reaffirm our faith in and constant reliance upon God…

Wisconsin 1848, We, the people of Wisconsin, grateful to Almighty God for our freedom, domestic tranquility.

Wyoming 1890, We, the people of the State of Wyoming, grateful to God for our civil, political, and religious liberties…establish this Constitution.

How do we feel now? Look how the American Civil Liberties Union (A.C.L.U.) has changed their agenda. The A.C.L.U. used to be a great thing, no more, now it has a very liberal agenda. This agenda is leading to socialism!

Chapter Three
Where is God?

We need God in our lives, we need to educate our children to know and love our God. If you are an Atheist or Agnostic, this is perfectly alright with me. I will respect you, but you in turn should respect my choices. We have never ever heard publicly a Christian or a Jewish person disrespecting an Atheist, at least I have not.

The last couple of Christmas's we have heard many cities and towns that wanted Christ taken out of Christmas. The media was all over this new and disgusting idea. Bans were made on Nativity scenes in many cities. Schools were calling the season, "holiday" or "winter" break rather than using the word Christmas break.

John Gibson wrote a book called <u>Christmas Under Attack;</u> think about it. How dare anyone attack my religious beliefs and our Christmas holiday. There is an awful man Newdau who used his daughter to attack the Pledge of Allegiance in her school. As of this writing, I do believe court appeals are still pending (this did go to the Supreme Court). If this misfit did not want his daughter to say the word God in the Pledge just have her not say God. As the story unfolded in the media this jerk was separated from his wife and daughter. His wife is raising the girl to be a Christian. His family does not condone his actions. The worst part about this whole story is how much media attention this jerk got. The A.C.L.U. was involved too. I personally know two people that are Agnostic. I have never and will never disrespect their ideas. They know that I disagree, and they respect my stand.

The A.C.L.U. was founded in 1920. Their agenda has never really changed, they spew untruths. I think the A.C.L.U. should either close their doors or perhaps it is high time to examine what they stand for.

They should leave religion, families and peoples personal choices alone. Enough is enough with "political correctness!"

Speaking of the media, I could fill a million pages. Very few media outlets report the news fair. ABC, MSNBC, CBS and NBC are so liberal and bias. It is so obvious in this 2008 election season. How can we condone the media hyping that disgusting dictator Hugo Chavez speaking at the United Nations and calling our President a devil? How do we condone the media to even cover the stories about the President of Iran? I know people need to know everything about everyone, but if you take the time to really listen to these bias newscasts you would understand my concerns. I have spoken to many people and sadly they do not watch the news. Most young people know nothing or very little about what is going on in our country and why things are happening. That my friends is a sad commentary.

Look at what happened a few months ago. The President of Iran said he wanted to wipe Israel off the map and refers to the United States of America as the great Satan. What do we do? We put him on the cover of TIME magazine. What is wrong with us? Why haven't we all cancelled our subscriptions to TIME magazine? Put these people out of business, we can do that one cancellation at a time. Newsweek is awful! Time to cancel that magazine too! We have the right to disagree with our President, and all that is wrong in our country. But come on folks, never allow outsiders to do the same. It is very simple, it is called respect. Is that what we want young people to learn and know in their lives? If you are that unhappy with your country leave, move to another country.

Remember Barbara Streisand making the comment "if George Bush becomes president I will move out of the country" (I mentioned this earlier). Well guess what, she is still here. The USA has made her a star and a millionaire. That is the real reason she remains here. George W. Bush is a Christian, maybe that is the real reason why so many secular progressives hate him. I was offended by her remarks. I threw all her CDs in the garbage. She is one of the greats but I will never spend my American dollars on her.

The left wing nuts in Hollywood are sickening. We already discussed Michael Moore and his kind, and all of Hollywood is entitled to lean any way they want. But to call your standing president a liar, stupid, ignorant and much more to me is un-American and unpatriotic. Not only are we hearing all this ignorance the entire world is also hearing it. What have we as American's become when we go to other countries and speak so poorly about our sitting president and our government? Where did all this hate come from? How can our children learn the correct way of life when they hear this kind of hate? I actually heard a seven year old child say, "I hate the president" why would a loving caring parent allow this? The answer is simple. They do not care! Those kinds of people are not patriots. Again it goes back to the media. We can only hope things get better because I do not think they can sink much lower than they are now.

Internet Hate

Have you seen some of the hate blogs on the internet? You would be amazed at all the lies and unproven facts and just plain gossip. How does this happen? Yes folks, freedom of speech is in our great country! We as American's should start acting like American's, boycott this evil on the internet. Let us not accept what is unhealthy in our country. As I stated to you about bad judges…say no! Get rid of them! Say no to newspapers, cancel them, I have! Magazines, blogs any media that spews ugly bias news. No matter what political views you have, RESEARCH and make good wise decisions. Remember we are American's first and formost make your decisions as an American! Not a republican, democrat or independent.

Let me list some junk for you to think about.

November 2006 democrats took over the Congress. We American's were promised the world. We voted them in and look at what they have done. Absolutely nothing, broken promises.

November 2006, the city of San Francisco bans the ROTC.

November 2006 college in Casa Mesa California bans the pledge of allegiance. UNAMERICAN!

November 2006 O.J. Simpson gets a book published telling the world how he would have killed his wife and Ron Goldman. Only in America can this happen.

November 2006 violence at retail stores from people waiting in line to buy the latest toy (the latest toy…think about that fact).

November 2007 yet another liberal judge in Missouri gives sex offender probation.

Oops guess what? I just heard we win one for our side; the book of O.J. Simpson's will not make the bookshelves.

2007 Rosie O'Donnell tells the world that 9/11 was the makings of the USA. I knew she was not long on the View, Hooray!

December 2007 six Muslim men were arrested because of a ruckus on an American Airline plane. Now I will watch this mess and I hope you are also watching. ACLU was involved in this and called it "profiling." I have many more news items for you to see in the coming chapters. I want you to be aware of what is happening in our country.

Chapter Four
Our Kids

What is going on with our young people today? Lets take a closer look at just what is going on with today's youngsters. Where are the moms and dads when their teen daughters leave the house for school in the mornings? Does anyone notice how their teens and younger kids are dressed? Who buys them these clothes? What are parents thinking when they allow their kids to wear inappropriate outfits? Would any parent want their daughter to look like a slut? Another thing that bothers me is boys who wear their pants down around their knees with their underwear hanging out. Dress codes in schools are a good thing.

Why would a parent want their daughter to be popular with the boys at ages like 12, 13, and 14? I have heard parents talk like that. Lets get back to the good old days when girls did not sleep around. When oral sex was unacceptable and not talked about. The younger the girls are dating the more sexually active they will become. That is a fact! Enter the new culture of kids out of control. I am sorry to say, you parents have caused it. Where are you that you do not have a clue what your kids are doing, where they are going and what they are learning? Girls as young as 11 having babies!

Remember how Miss America last year went wild? The media covered that story and she was given a second chance. Wow! What message is the world sending to our young people? She should have lost her crown. That would have been the proper message.

Let me list some facts that you may already know.

April 2008: young pre-teens 12 years old beating each other with rocks and filming the beating for You Tube. Where are the parents?

27

April 2008: California boy age 9 on a hip-hop website threatening sniper attacks. This boy has eight minutes of insane rants. How do we handle this? Where are the parents?

In the same month, Miley Cyrus age 15, idol of your young daughters has racy internet photos posted. This young icon is worth millions because of us, you and me! Miley is Disney's biggest star. Once again we have no heroes.

April 2007: Murder plot foiled, young girls planning a murder and how to dispose of the body. These girls are 13 and 14 years old. They were referring to murdering a classmate. This took place in a middle school in Kentucky. A parent tipped off the school. I wish I knew more about this story, somehow a parent was there and got involved. Hooray!

December 2007: Young girls beating a young man on a New York subway. Again posted on You Tube!

Lets face it young people are not being taught good judgment. Are they looking for attention? Are they looking for affirmation? Just simply being loved is what they need.

June 2008: Full nudity on the internet, photos taken with cell phones and posted on the internet. These girls are ages 11, 12, and 13. First of all what are they doing with cell phones? Again I must ask where are the parents? The reality is (and I say this with sadness) the parents simply do not care.

June 2008: By now the world knows about the so called "pregnancy pact" in Glouschester Massachusetts. 17 high school girls getting pregnant on purpose. What the hell is going on in that town? As the

28

days have passed and I watch the news coverage I cannot believe this story. The school starts to hand out pregnancy tests but does not hand out contraceptives. Please someone explain to me how 17 sets of parents have missed all the signs of this situation unfolding? What a pity for the babies of these young girls. Again one of the pregnant girls and her boyfriend were guests on one of the mainstream TV shows. Being celebrated. Any parent with any common sense has to be horrified. Pictures of these girls were shown while they were strolling up and down the halls at school. This school also has a daycare center for the babies. Where is our world heading? There used to be a stigma associated to a pregnant teen, not anymore! I say too bad. Some of the fathers of these babies are teens themselves, some are not. Is that not rape if the father is over 18? The superintendent of the school has remarked that some of these girls have low self-esteem. He also said that most had no love or direction in their lives. Where will this road lead? According to this superintendent, not one parent has even called the school. This my friends is not that uncommon today. One school reported 90 pregnant girls in one particular high school.

November 2007: 13 year old Megan Meyer commits suicide (another teens parent) bullied her on her My Space.

June 2008: Quebec Canada. A father is being sued by his 12-year-old child because he punished her. The girl was taken away from her computer because she posted inappropriate pictures of herself on the internet. The judge overruled the parent. Do you see where the future is headed? As long as we have bad judges and the ACLU, this is just the beginning.

June 2008: Oregon principle bans the pledge of allegiance because it might offend the Muslims. The seculars are winning in this country! Be careful!

June 2008: another story of youngsters in Bergan county New Jersey. Ninth grade girls posing topless and sending the pictures over their cell phones. Parents wake up! Some high schools are looking to a dress code for prom dresses. Think about that! Why would parents allow their daughters to dress inappropriately to attend their prom?

Everyday we hear about female teachers having sex with students. We are not even shocked anymore. Teachers posing on the internet. How has all this happened in our society? Parents you must examine yourselves. The ethics and values are a total mess in this country.

Another shocking story related to the internet has just caught my interest. Kids are going to drive through fast food windows ordering large drinks then throw the drink into the face of the employee who just waited on them. This whole stupid mess was filmed and posted on the internet. Can you imagine your child doing that? I can't! Some stupid parents remarked, "at least no weapon was used, just kids being kids." "No big deal."

April 2008: a 16 year old boy was plotting on-line to have a Columbine type of attack and was looking for people to do simultaneous attacks on September 11, 2008. Fortunately this young man is in custody as we speak. This boy had in his room over 100 knives. Once again, where are the parents? Any real parent would know their child owns 100 knives.

April 2008: Boca Raton Florida, another campus shooting. A fight breaks out at a party a gun was pulled out and fired. Thank God no victims this time.

Nine kids between the ages of 8 and 10 in Georgia were plotting to kill their teacher. They had weapons, duct tape, and a carefully laid out plan. No charges were pressed because of the kids ages. All the kids were released to their parents. Now what? I would love to know one of these kids ten years from now!

Since December 2007 we are aware of 10 teacher student scandals. The ages of these teachers range from 28 to 42. Most of them are in there 30s. Most of these women are good looking and shapely. What possible kick can they get with a young boy? The boys "victims" have me a little perplexed as well. I believe these boys are loving this whole thing. Remember any young boy should already know how wrong this is. Child psychologist Gail Cross claims most parents are uncooperative. Do not get me wrong I want these teachers prosecuted. The numbing of our morals in this county is outrageous!

February 14: two school shootings in one week one in North Illinois and one in Louisiana. Fifteen students dead sixteen injured. The Louisiana Tech shooter was a girl! Surprise, surprise! Colorado shooting in a school, this young man had a shotgun. The shotgun was apprehended but the 15 year old ran into the principles office with a handgun and shot the principle three times. Less than a week later another head case walks into an Amish school and slaughters several young girls. This man was older. Hearing all of this I remember

Columbine. Why has all this senseless and awful behavior become so popular?

April 2008: The largest school shooting in the history of the United States. The Virginia Tech gunman wounded 22 and I believe he killed 20 people. Then he turned the gun on himself. Is anyone safe anymore? Why has our society become this violent? I believe with all my heart it starts in the home. Even some really nice people have a bad seed among them. But I think a parent can recognize a problem in his child if that parent is fully aware and takes the time to notice. When they do notice they can help that child.

August 2008: a 17 year old boy in Cleveland carjacks a car, but before the drives away he beats the car owner to a pulp. The man was 91 years old. The man was all right and the carjacker was caught and arrested. What kind of troubled youth would beat a 91 year old? What kind of rage is in that young mans heart and head? Check the parents you and will see why!

June 2008: Missing child Brooke Bennetts body was found near her uncles home in Vermont. Maybe you heard this awful story. The child was reported missing and her picture was all over the news. I was sure it was some kind of internet thing. It was not. It was some awful sex club her uncle was to initiate her into. All the facts are not out yet so a lot of facts are still missing. However, the uncle lured the girl while using the internet. I knew the internet was involved! Tell me why this young girl is on My Space? Why is any youngster under the age of 15 on My Space? It is truly a terrible story. The state of Vermont is the location. After watching the investigation and learning how many times this man was charged and convicted of rape, served little time and is branded a sex offender, again a bad Judge!

Again we see how bad these liberal judges are. Vermont does not have Jessicas Law. It is time for the people of Vermont to step up to the plate. We know nothing much about the parents of this poor child. But I would have to believe the worst. I am sorry for that. But someone has failed that child. Bill O'Reilly's book Culture Warrior discussed the weak leaders and chaotic legislature in Vermont. O'Reilly ripped a judge Cashman in Vermont for the very lenient sentence he gave to child rapists. There it is again folks, a bad judge! Vermont is not the only state with bad judges. Do yourself a favor, and Google the 9th circuit court. You will witness liberal judges like you have never seen before. This should not be!

I am personally tickled to death that the media is all over missing children. Besides Jessica's Law we have the Amber Alert and several other laws on the books. All states must and should get moving to pass these laws and follow up on them. All of the young people, by nature, are susceptible to bad judgments. We know this up front, so all I really want you as the parent to do is watch, listen, and simply be aware. The internet is dangerous. Strangers are dangerous. Nothing in the world is more important than the well being of your children. Become proactive. Do your job with gusto!

Chapter Five
The Media

I know we have already discussed the liberal media but I want to let you know some facts that have taken place this year and last.

August 2008: The very liberal New York Times reports, "The nation is in decline, the neglect in this country is stunning." Listing all the declines.

Politicians are corrupt, schools and collages are way too liberal. The media is whacked out! What to do? Lets list some of the facts we know. California passed a new law allowing prison inmates conjugal visits. How sweet!

From May 2007 to June 2007 The New York Times ran several stories about plots of Muslims to kill Americans. Nine Muslims have been arrested. All the stories were buried in the newspaper. These stories should be front- page news. We Americans need to know!

Hospitals all over the United States are filthy! Yes, you heard me it is a universal problem. Not enough money to keep them clean. Look at what we are paying in hospital insurance; according to the experts it is just not enough! So many people die each year because of infections picked up in the hospital. Emergency rooms all over the country are filthy. In my research on this subject, I have come up with nine different stories. We can complain everyday and nothing will change. Some top guns have told me it is all political. Can this be true? I think this subject could be a whole other book.

Commercials

Here are some disturbing commercials. Daughter goes to Dad and asks for $85.00 to buy a pair of jeans. The dad asks his teen if her friends have the same jeans, she answers yes. The Dad proceeds to go on-line to check it out. After he sees the jeans on-line he proceeds to hand her the $85.00. The commercial is for some investment company. Am I stupid or did I miss the whole point of that commercial?

We watch at least four commercials about erectile dysfunction. Give me a break! Every man in these commercials seems way too young to have erectile dysfunction. There are so many wild commercials, but my final two will make you stop and reflect.

PETA has a commercial out with a mom and dad telling their teen daughter to have sex and lots of it. The daughter says, "but what if I become pregnant?" The parents proceed to tell her they will find a home for the babies or just let them run loose on the streets. The point I guess was "have your pets spayed or neutered." Can you even imagine your teenage daughter seeing this? Thankfully this commercial was taken off the air.

The final commercial is to me, shattering! "Total Transformation System." This is for enrollment to a program to be able to transform your very bad and uncooperative child into a model child. Their claim is you will see a change in just two weeks! Even if your child has attention deficit disorder (A.D.D.) or attention deficit hyperactivity disorder (A.D.H.D.). Wow! After this program we will never see another bad child on this earth! Just call 1-800-blah-blah-blah. How about you call me 1-800-Gloria, I will not hesitate to tell you to take over your child's life for one week. He or she will straighten out or else. Think about this ad parents, do you need this sort of crap to raise your child?

Does anyone really care about people like Jerry Springer, Rosie O'Donnell, Paris Hilton, Lindsay Lohan, Brittany Spears and many others? Obviously some people do because every single magazine cover shows these people front and center. Go figure! Here are more news stories that were not on the front page.

May 2007: five men plotting to kill Americans at Fort Dix, three of these men were in our country illegally. News front page of the same paper: Mother telling her daughter to fight on school bus. News front page: Another teacher sending love letters to underage student. News: this report buried inside the newspaper: three children 8 years old and younger left home alone. The 8 year old calls 911. Police arrive and confiscate drugs and drug paraphernalia.

Here is one that will make you cringe. June 2007 The New York Times wrote about the thwarted plot of New Jersey men planning to blow up JFK Airport. The article was on page 37. The New York Times hates Bush and the administration so much they just cannot help themselves. Front page news: Kids are too fat in America, we all know that don't we? And we who are sensible even know why. No one plays outside anymore. Too much fast food, no parents monitoring what their children are eating. All of you parents that really care know what to do.

May 2008: website defacing the Jenna Bush wedding. My question is why?

The TV show Boston Legal spewing hate about President Bush. Why?

Hamas TV. Ok folks, this is not an American TV station. But some fool thought it was just fine to show the excerpts. One part shows a child stabbing President Bush repeatedly (this is a children's show) thus, showing President Bush begging for their forgiveness. In this show it shows the White House as a Mosque. This is just a small part of the Muslims teachings. They teach their children hate and to kill the infidels. The United States of America is the infidel. Our great country cares about Muslims. I do not understand why.

April 2008: California teacher tells his students "when you put your Jesus glasses on you can't see the truth."

A teacher in Capistrano California was constantly making disparaging remarks about Christianity. A Federal judge is looking at this case. I will follow up on that one. Hopefully this is not just another liberal judge.

Anti-American rally's everywhere. Americans are screaming about the poor souls in Guantanamo Bay. Not one of these people lost a loved one in a terrorist attack or a son or daughter serving our country.

These are liberal do-gooders who need to wake up and love their country or leave it! The prisoners in Gitmo are being treated well. They have their own special foods. They eat better than our military.

We now have a website to tell you (and your children) how to enjoy sex. This website will help you do "what needs to be done." We have another website that will help predators find little boys and girls. This website leads one through the process of all the know-hows, even where to find these kids. Isn't that wonderful? Is this freedom or what? We have many websites out there that will teach you how to make bombs. Our country is in a moral freefall!

May 2008: Cell phones taped a teacher-student brawl at a high school near Atlanta. Teacher was a substitute.

April 2008: Rapper 50 Cent and girlfriend fighting over a home he supposedly promised her and their 8 year-old Son. Guess what, the house burned to the ground. Hmm!

May 2008: A prom night in a high school in Memphis Tennessee filmed on You Tube. Teachers (chaperones) stood by and watched young people simulating sex. The chaperones merely stood by and watched. Shame on them! Home is where we learn what we live! I just learned this practice is called "grinding" OK!

April 2008: A student in Baltimore Maryland filmed by another student beating an art teacher.

April 2008: 28 students in Farmington Utah trade nude pictures with each other's boyfriends. Their ages were between 13 & 15.

April 2008: We all have heard the story from Florida where 6-8 girls lured a friend to one of their homes. The intention was to beat her and videotape the beating so they can put it on the internet. Some of the girls have been charged as adults.

Believe me, I could tell you a dozen more stories like these. But I think I have more than made my point. I hope you really learned what is going on. Do not bury your heads in the sand. It is not good out there!

Chapter Six
Politics

2008 Elections

By the time this book is printed we will have a new President in the White House. And I for one am scared out of my mind. We are down to the wire with Barack Obama and John McCain. I am a republican. But I will tell you that all of my life I have voted both ways. I try to learn as much as I can and I try to vote wisely. I have voted for democrats many times so I hope you can see where I am coming from.

I am watching this long drawn out campaign for the last year. I have learned much and I will share some with you. I was amazed reading what each candidate has spent in this campaign. They have spent millions and millions of dollars to tell you and me lies, distortions, and just plain nonsense. Can you imagine the good those dollars could do in our towns and cities. All the candidates running are senators. Now you know each of them gets a salary of about $165,000 per year. We pay their salary. They work for us.

Obama and McCain have been campaigning for about a year now. They are doing nothing in our "do nothing" Congress and Senate. Can you imagine any of us taking the year off to run for office and still get paid? What is wrong with this picture? They should take a pay-cut in their absence. Did you know Barack Obama has only spent 156 days as a Senator?

I do think they worked hard to become elected. I will also admit I admire their stamina. I do not discount the process however. We need truth! We need kept promises! We need to really believe in the person who will be our commander and chief. Having said that, how many are really honest? There are very few in my opinion. This election is historic because we have a black man running. In the democratic party we have speaker of the house Nancy Pelosi telling lie after lie. She hates President Bush so much I do not think she can help herself. Pelosi tells the world we need dialog with other countries. We need truth in our country. My question to her is to care about her own constituency and the American people first. She and many more of them are so full of hate they cannot and will not do the right thing. And remember she is third in line to become President.

As I said before when the democrats took over congress in 2006? They made a million promises and kept none. Pelosi said we will do it all in the first 100 days. They did not. They have crippled Congress.

I am around young people a lot and I try to listen to their thoughts about their favorite candidates. I must say it is pretty frightening. I ask, "tell me why you like Obama." The answer is always "because he wants change." "What change" I ask. They usually cannot give me an answer. I usually hear some rambling about the war. They do not understand no President alone can end the war by a finger snap.

Young people do not follow the real news. They go to blogs. Big mistake! Blogs can make them believe anything. In this campaign season all the mainstream media is backing Barack Obama. You will not get a fair and balanced attitude on those shows. Some believe John McCain is too old to be President. I strongly disagree. The people our age, John and I, are brilliant compared to the young men and women today. We have something very unique and special to offer our country. That something is wisdom. We "oldies" have been around a long time. We have seen it all. Why aren't these young people paying attention to us? I for one do not want a new young President. Especially the one on this ticket. He has no real life experience and hardly any in the Senate. I truly hope who ever gets into the White House will institute a lot of changes.

We need so much in this country and we as Americans need to pay attention. I believe we will be at war in the Middle East for a very long time. I believe Iran is next, than Syria and on and on. I hope I am wrong!

Let's talk about the Supreme Court of the United States. Look what those people go through just to be vetted. Shouldn't the American people do the same for President? We need a conservative Supreme Court. We need a conservative Congress. We need a conservative Senate. We need a conservative President. But if I as an American do not get my way, than please just give me reasonable men and women who care for all the people. Especially our kids!

America first. English language first. No more illegals. Lets close those borders so we can sort out all the problems we face today. Of course we welcome immigrants here but they must do it legally. Like my grandparents did.

We need to clean up our great country. We need to begin with a moratorium on immigration. We need to get rid of the criminals who are illegal. We have our own American criminals to worry about.

Let's talk a bit about all the sordid problems with so many members of Congress and dirty Senators. Every other week we hear a new story. I ask myself " were these people always dirty or did the job change them?" Big egos, who, like Bill Clinton, do what they do because THEY CAN.

I think we are not paying attention to who we are electing. As I have said before check these people out before you elect them. With the internet you can. You can e-mail your Congressmen and Senators. You can let them know how you feel about anything. I have said before and I will say it again "become proactive!" You must start paying attention. Do it for the kids!

My final thought on this subject is our hope for a better tomorrow depends on your vote for the next President. Whoever wins this 2008 election has a lot of work to do. I pray our next President is not Obama. He is not what we need to lead us. Trust my wisdom on this one!

Chapter Seven
Race

Race in the United States

Do we still have a problem with race in this country? Yes, we do. I am convinced that white people have come a long way. But I am also convinced that black people have not. Let me explain. We the white people have tried to do our job to stop the use of the "N" word and pay attention to "affirmative action." We the white people have tried to be "politically correct" in dealing with black people. We hear the black leaders like Al Sharpton and Jessie Jackson talking about the "poor black man" in jail. They want to know why there are 75 percent more blacks incarcerated than whites. Is it at all possible that black men have perpetrated more crimes than the white man? Hello!

We watched for almost one year the famous Duke case. These three white lacrosse players were slammed. They were called racist, kidnappers, and thugs. After all they were accused of raping a black woman. I for one, felt if all was true lock them up. All three were acquitted. This story was front-page news for about a year. Those three young men's lives were at a standstill. The so-called victim was nowhere. Their families were tortured and the word racists was thrown around like crazy. Jesse Jackson and Al Sharpton were all over this case.

About the same time that same year a white male and a white female were kidnapped, raped, sodomized and brutally killed by five black men. I am not positive where this took place because the media was terrible in their reporting I believe it was in North Carolina. The coverage was so sparse I could not believe it. We heard nothing from the real racists, Al Sharpton or Jesse Jackson.

All I could think at the time was why don't we, the white folks, have our leaders out their yelling "foul." The reason is we do not want to be called racists. It is time we the white (elite), as they like to call us, step up to the plate and start screaming "racists" every time we need to. The left wing media is doing more harm than good in this arena.

We are sorry, truly sorry blacks were slaves 100 years ago. Today is 2008 and the blacks have come a long way. I for one am proud to see a Colin Powell, Condoleezza Rice, and Clarence Thomas as leaders. My question is where are the real black leaders in the small communities? Why do we have so many gangs? Why is the young black girl having babies one after the other out of wedlock? So many of the black homes are single mother only homes. These black girls are uneducated and more than not are living with their single uneducated mother. Where is the good parent? Where are the leaders of the black communities?

Bill Cosby has been outspoken on this very subject for a long time. He wants his people to get their act together. Even he is criticized by his own people. Has the racial divide closed in this country? My answer is not enough! Frankly as a taxpayer I am tired of it all. As long as our government is handing out the checks not much will change. And that goes for the whites as well. Where are the leaders who need to say, "go to work, stop getting pregnant, stop blaming the white man, and simply take responsibility."

I humbly believe the reason we are still discussing this so called "race issue" is because the whites are letting it happen. If the white community would stand up and scream racist every time they are discriminated against things would change.

Think about O.J. Simpson for a minute. Any rational person on the face of this earth knows the man was and still is guilty of murder. I wonder if the race card was not used how many sane blacks would feel different. Race was the number one priority in that murder case. Until the black people understand that in this great country all children can get an education. All people can achieve, black or white. Any child can learn to read and write. Just stay in school.

I do not believe things will change in my lifetime, but I pray they can in yours. What I see from my small corner of the world is wonderful, hard working black families. To me, they are the absolute same human beings as the white hardworking families. But I am sad to say I see also the militant blacks that are out of control. Yes, there is the same element in the white militant. But I truly believe the blacks out number the whites.

I wish all black people would just simply put the word "slavery" out of their vocabulary. Raise their children to respect all people. Give their children the confidence to be what ever they want to be. God in their lives is so important. I bet if we did a comparison in black families who are Christians, Jews or any other religion, they are better families.

I for one am very tired of being told that black children do not have the same opportunities as whites do. Because folks they do! One of my doctors is a black woman. I cannot tell you the respect I have for her. Any black child has the advantage to become anything she or he aspires to be.

We now have a black man running for the White House. Is that not wonderful? Every black man and woman in this country should be proud. Twenty years ago you never saw black ladies and gentlemen on commercials, TV shows and more importantly, judges, mayors, senators or congressmen. I feel we have come a long way.

Chapter Eight
Respect

In my first book <u>Hit Them Harder</u> I went into the topic of respect. What I wanted to get across on this subject was how the idea of respect begins at home. Children watch and learn what they live from a very early age. The parents, you, are the teachers. If you do not respect each other what can you expect your children to learn? Just respecting each other by doing all the everyday manners does not cut it. It is how you treat your elderly, parents and friends. It is how you refer to fire fighters, police officers, and the President of the United States. Your references to those people is learned by your children.

Let us examine this topic. You are the parent and you say thank you at stores, restaurants, and to all service people. Trust me your kids will pick all that up. You just telling them to say please and thank you is not enough. You must do this at home on a daily basis. I have actually seen parents of teenagers remind them to say please and thank you. Lets face it, if your teen has to be reminded every day, you have failed.

I recently read a book written by Thomas Sowall, the book is named <u>A Man on Letters</u>. This author claims "I am not sure the United States can be saved." What he is referring to is the terrible society we are living in; the lack of respect for our government and families falling apart. Young people making extremely bad decisions, our young parents today in their thirties and forties are so oblivious to what is going on in our world.

Never forget the children we are referring to will be the leaders of our country twenty years from now. I have yet to meet a young person I could say would be a great leader someday. There is one I can think of my granddaughter Samantha. She is 13 years old and her ambition and tenacity has overwhelmed me.

One young man told me recently his 14 year old daughter came home from school and told her parents how much she hated the president. Lack of respect? Yes and yes again. This sort of thing should never enter the classroom. What did those parents do? Nothing, afraid to rock the boat. How unfortunate. It is bad enough all the collage professors are spewing all sorts of liberal garbage to our young people and getting away with it.

Forget for a moment the manners that should be taught. Let us talk of the disrespect shown to our country. Ripping apart our great country. I have mentioned some already but here is a few more to think about. Jane Fonda using the "C" word on national TV. Drug addicted Amy Winehouse wins all kinds of awards at the Grammys, and proceeds to use all kinds of obscenities in her slurred acceptance speech. Sally Fields whom I have always liked, not any more. She uses the podium at the no longer acceptable Oscars to use profane words against the present administration. Diane Keaton another one using the "F" word on TV. Rappers using this trash and filth in their lyrics. What has happened to us? If you or your child respects these disrespectful people you as the parent are loosing the battle.

Montessori schools have the students call the teachers by their first names! The administration believes this action teaches mutual respect. Spare me!

When did all this begin? Well, the answer is in your home. You do not have to like anyone, especially those people representing your city, state and country. What you have most is a responsibility to get involved. Remove the people in office by your vote. Teach your children to also learn what theses people are all about. A simple click on the computer can tell them. After all, they spend hours on the computer anyway.

How do we overcome all the negative respect surrounding us. From the day your baby is born until adulthood you alone are their teachers of respect and values. If you do the job early on, it will become easier as they grow. Will they change the rules and opinions you taught them? Of course they will. After all they have minds of their own. But no matter where they go and what they become reverts back to where they were.

It takes a lot of energy to always do and say the right thing. As normal loving parents you will lose a few but persistent consistency and living what you teach them will make your child a better person.

I promise you this, every child learns what he lives and if your home is filled with love, values and respect you will love the outcome.

Chapter Nine
Patriotism

What does patriotism mean? I suppose it could mean different things to different people. But I will tell you what it means to me. If you are a true God loving American you love your country unconditionally. This does not mean you feel all the ills of our administration, government are correct. You have the perfect right to question any and all that goes on in our country.

You can get angry from time to time and be upset over decisions made and you can even speak out against your Presidents and government. But having said all that a true American will never go to a foreign country and knock America. A true American will never, ever burn the flag of our great country.

Universities all over this great land employ professors who, to me are unpatriotic and un-American. Liberals are fine, it is the far left that is spewing hate filled messages to our young men and women in college.

How does a university condone inviting the President of Iran to speak? Hate filled students carrying signs. What happened to what they have learned at home? Perhaps not learned at home. Remember back in September 2007 when General Petraeus was grilled before Congress about the war in Iraq? The next day The New York Times printed a funded by the left hate group "Move On.Org", and referred to the General as General "betray us." This my friends is not only unpatriotic, it is anti-American. General Petraeus is great man serving his country.

In a Boulder Colorado high school, students walked out of school refusing to say the Pledge of Allegiance. Where are the parents of these kids? There is an attack on religion in this country and in my view that alone is un-American. The secular progressives are running wild. Why don't these people who hate America just quietly move to another country? It is really so simple, pick up your belongings and move.

All I want to say to you on this topic is, it all happens in the home. Talk to your kids when you hear or read about some stupid secular person denouncing your country or see some anti-American burning a flag. Let your family speak freely about what they hear in class. What went on in Boulder is going on all around us. Do we believe in freedom of speech? Of course we do. Thank God we live in a country that allows us the right to speak free. But when you denounce your country you are unpatriotic and it is as simple as that. Take pride in your country display a flag. Encourage your kids to know about their forefathers.

What is socialism? "Public collective ownership or control of the basic means of production, distribution and exchange. Assuring to each member of society an equitable share of goods, services, and welfare benefits." Do you want socialism? Socialized medicine, is this the direction our country is heading in? If Barack Obama is our next president you will see it come. Americans are not meant to be socialists!

I can not confirm this next statement, but I do believe a lot of our schools have cut back on the old ways of teaching history. I have heard this time and time again from teachers. Ask your child, it seems kids today are learning less and less about the history of our country. Isn't that a shame? God Bless America.

Chapter Ten
Angelo's Pizzeria

Two of my sons own a pizzeria restaurant in a lovely and growing young community. Since they opened their doors almost seven years ago I have worked there. I am a "certified waitress" because I like people and love to talk and express my opinions. I really have enjoyed my job. I love being around my sons as well.

While I was growing up my family never went out to eat. Back in those prehistoric days not many restaurants were around. I sure remember the first McDonalds opening in our town. A hamburger was twenty cents. You could not eat inside and there was no such thing as drive thru.

Dinner was always at the table and all the family members were required to attend. If a family member was missing for one reason or another his/her dinner was kept on the stove and warmed for him/her when they arrived home. We had no microwave ovens back then.

After I grew up and married, the same path was followed, dinner every night. If Dad worked late, as my husband often did, he was fed a warm dinner when he got home. No matter what time it was. I was always happy to serve him.

Dinner in our home and everyone else I knew was meat, potatoes, vegetables, salad, bread and butter and most of the time a good dessert. Of course the meat was also substituted with chicken or fish. But be assured it was always full courses. Thursdays and Sundays were pasta nights. Milk was big in our home, four growing boys to fill up. Never unless I was having company did I even buy pop. I remember my sons loving when company was coming they knew they could grab a can of pop. Juice was also a big deal in our home. Snacks were peanut butter and jelly and fruit was always on hand.

When my boys were growing up we hardly ever went out to eat. Our big outing with the kids was the local pancake house after church on Sundays.

My sons were hooligans, I am sure they remember all the threats, smacks, and pinches (high underneath the armpit) they received. Somehow they always made us proud in public. When we arrived home all hell broke loose (the horns popped out)!

As I stated in my book Hit Them Harder we parents can learn a lot about your child at the blessed dinner table. For some unknown reason kids always spill the beans at the table. It is usually by pure accident and small talk. Parents if your not around the table most nights of the weeks, you are truly missing a lot. I realize it is a different time now, kids are involved in a million activities and sports. But again I will tell you if you wanted to you could fit the dinner table in that busy schedule! Our families were busy back in the "old days." My boys were involved in all the sports and you name it they did it. Times have not changed that much.

Another important point is vitamins for kids. Many parents I talk to do not push their child towards the daily vitamin. Every morning of my children's lives the vitamin bottle was on the breakfast table. One young mom told me her doctor said they do not need vitamins. That could be true, but still what could it hurt? To me kids need them far more today than they did all those years ago. Today kids are eating poorly. Fact: the children of today will be the most unhealthy adults in the history of this country.

Our family pizzeria is a child friendly restaurant catering to families. What I am about to tell you about our customers will blow you away or maybe not. What I have seen is not good news, if I listed every little story I could fill many pages. I will list a few to give you an idea of what I see every single day. I want you as parents to see what is going on with your parenting skills!

I believe our culture is at a very steep decline. The kids, your kids are running your homes. The inmates are running the asylum.

A parent with two small kids ages 2 and 4, the parent was there alone. When I asked for their order the dad shushed me and told me to wait until the commercial came on the TV. This man would not interrupt his kids so I could take their order. I walked away literally shaking my head in disbelief. Can you just imagine for a moment the waitress waiting for the commercial so these very young kids can order? Maybe I should get rid of the TV. But the customers can always turn it off.

We also have a jukebox in the restaurant and to make a selection you keep clicking as the CDs appear. The process can be very noisy and if you happen to be sitting close to the jukebox, it can be very annoying. We placed a sign on the front of the box asking kids not to play with the jukebox. Little kids (who can not read) will stand there and simply click away. Parents can read (I think), so why do they allow it to happen and say nothing until I ask the child not to play with the jukebox. The parents usually ignore the situation.

Okay!

A few months ago a bunch of boys about the ages of 12 or 13 were having ice cream outside came in the dining room to use the restrooms. That evening the dining room was busy, a lot of people were eating dinner. After the boys made a lot of noise entering the dining room several went directly to the jukebox while each boy used the restroom. The boys were loud and disturbing customers while pressing the buttons on the jukebox. Finally, I said "hey guys, please don't play with the jukebox." One of the boys stepped back and gave me the up and down look of disrespect. The boy was mumbling some nasty remarks and turned and stomped out of the restaurant. A few minutes later, he walks back in with a smug look on his face and his 6 foot dad at his side. The dad walks up to me really close and says "do we have a problem" in a very nasty tone of voice. I lost total control of my senses. I moved in even closer to him, jabbed my finger in his chest and told him to "get out!" I was beet red and shaken up. Both father and son had an attitude it was obvious.

Now what message was that action by the father to his smug faced son? I thought about it all night long. I feel sad for that boy.

Three little kids about ages 4 and 5 were running around the dining room screaming and laughing while the parents say and do nothing. I have to tell the kids to sit down. This is a common occurrence in our dining room. These kids are being disruptive to other diners and their parents do not even care. Tell me folks what are they thinking? Many families put their kids at separate tables. What is that about?

Always and forever kids will spill. What does the average parent do? Nothing! What does a caring parent do? They give the waitress a hand in the cleanup. Our job is the cleanup but when a parent cares it is a pleasant task. I actually witnessed a child push his milk over, after I cleaned the mess, his mom told me to bring him another glass of milk. The child wanted pop and his parent's had said "no." Well guess what that boy did when the second milk was delivered? You guessed it, he knocked that one over as well. No refill was mentioned again, but I charged them for two glasses of milk. When the parents of this nasty child got the bill they questioned the charge for the two milks. By that time I could have cared less, I did not even dignify them with an answer. I feel sorry for that child, it is not his fault he is so nasty. What will his childhood be like? What will his time in school be like?

This next story is a favorite of mine. Several families come in who really are my favorites. However, every time these families come in they are constantly reminding their children to say please and thank you. They really do not realize it is too late these kids are from the ages of 8 to 16. Sometimes I say "what's the magic word?" my reasoning is to alert the parents. I have also found the rudest kids are the most demanding. The parents have forgotten to teach them even the smallest amount of respect for their server.

We have the families whose children do not eat. The parents threaten the child if they do not eat the server will not let them have dessert. The server can you believe it! The lazy parent wants me to be in charge? Most of this type of parent does not keep their word. The kid knows he will get dessert because that child knows his parents are weak. My hat goes out to the parents who do keep their word.

It is so heartwarming to wait on the families that are doing it the right way. I always compliment those parents. I am sorry to tell you that from my experience the good parents are in the minority. We also have the kids that spit paper at their siblings. Straw wrappers will be all over the floor. Parents are oblivious.

And what is with the text messaging and cell phones ringing in the dining room? This my friends is what the kids and parents are doing. Let me ask the question to you parents. Why does your 9-13 year old kids need a cell phone? Please do not tell me it is for their safety. When and where would those age kids ever be that you as a parent have no control? Where would they be that unsafe? Forget the rudeness of an adult talking on a cell phone while eating dinner with his family, what about a kid doing the same? In my humble opinion, these actions have really gone over the line. Nothing can be so important you have your cell on while eating in a restaurant. I have had customers let me wait for them to end their stupid phone call to order dinner. When I see someone on their cell phone I stay away until they summon me to take their order. Young kids texting while eating and the parents are totally oblivious.

You cannot imagine what parents allow their child to do. Recently I walked up to a table and noticed a slice of pizza turned upside down on the floor next to a boy about 10. I had no idea if the parent knew, so I asked the boy to please pick up the pizza. He just looked at me and so did the parents. I did bend down and pick it up. No comment from that table either.

Another favorite of mine is, one early evening while the dining room was filled. A blood curdling scream came from the ladies room. The little girl screaming was about 4. everyone in the dining room was quite, you could have heard a pin drop. The child was screaming "mommy" I looked over at the mom, who I noticed had decided to ignore the screams. Finally I walked up to her table where she was sitting with her husband and another couple and asked if that was her child. She replied yes and said she was ignoring her. I was stunned. I said "ignore her in your own home, please take care of this matter now, people are getting upset." She got up very annoyed and pulled the child out of the bathroom and began berating the child all through the dining room. The child never stopped crying and for the next half hour the parents continued to ignore her. People who were leaving the dining room were shaking their head.

What do you suppose those parents were trying to prove? To me and the rest of the customers, they proved just how bad their manners and respect for others are. Most importantly, how poor their parenting skills are. The father of that little girl never even looked up, what a wimp that dad was! Parents often ignore their crying child showing no respect for other diners. The good ones pick up their child or walk the child outside. I wonder how as a parent, you can just sit there and ignore a crying child.

Sometime ago I witnessed a young boy about 12 years old wait until his parents were out of sight and take a tip off the table. The tip was not my concern, I was upset that the boy stuffed it in his pocket. I decided I should tell his parents. I walked out the front door and called his mom aside. I told her what her son had done, the mother called the boy over and confronted him. He denied taking the tip. She turned to me and nicely said "you must be mistaken" I walked away feeling so sad. What is next for that young man?

Recently I watched as a 3 year old pulled a temper tantrum during dinner, not one tear visible. The mother was beside herself, she could not handle the child. She looked at me and said "she must be tired" I bet I get that comment at lease once a week. Being tired is no excuse for bad behavior mothers! If your child is tired stay home, make sure that child gets some rest.

Another family that comes in often, 5 young kids, are without a doubt a pleasure to wait on. This family has both parents working. But the parents have somehow accomplished the act of good training. They all have wonderful manners and know how to act in public I compliment them all the time.

I could tell you story after story about how kids behave in public. But I think you have the message. It is a wake up call to all parents. It is you the parent that has to take the bull by the horns. Good luck! Remember how you treat service people, your kids in turn will do the same. You are the teacher!

Chapter Eleven
Drugs

The bipolar epidemic is soaring in this country. Mental crisis. Is all this real? I do not know. Is the A.D.D. and A.D.H.D. real? I do not know. But what I do know are the facts. Today in our schools, more drugs are being used than ever in the history of this country by children in kindergarten through eighth grades. These drugs are lined up on the school nurses shelves. Keep in mind that doctors are funded by drug companies.

In our day the 60's and 70's, we as parents must have missed something because I know for sure everyone I knew had over rambunctious kids. As a mom of four very overactive boys they must have all had A.D.D. or A.D.H.D. All boys in my opinion are overactive. Today there are more child psychologists than ever before. Why? Back then we just parented.

Do you know that no long term studies have been done on the effects of all these drugs? I can spot a medicated kid a block away. Parents be very sure that your over active child is simply overactive. Do not be too quick to believe its more. Take time to double check with more than one doctor.

I am totally convinced that a lot of parents would rather have their child on some drug than spend the necessary time doing the hard work of parenting. It has also proven true that the medicated kid does not really eat properly, thus poor health. Parents please be sure your child really needs the medication he or she is taking. Again get several different opinions.

For the last few months and into the last year, we have been made aware of the famous athletes on steroids. Baseball has finally decided to work on this issue and I feel that it is about time.

Think about the implications of a popular athlete taking steroids. That is called cheating. Did you know that 60 percent of all students have admitted to cheating? We have watched the big guys making big bucks cheat.

I will never believe all the children on medication need those drugs. And as for you parents, demand a study to find out what the effects of those drugs will do to your child ten years from now. Again be aware and be proactive.

Chapter Twelve
Illegals

If you are keeping up with the news, you know all the stories about crime involving illegals. It seems that everyday we hear about a new crime.

The seculars want us the conservatives to be more politically correct in how we address illegals. They want us to refer to them as illegal immigrants or unauthorized workers and many other nicer phrases. I say no! they are what they are! Illegal aliens! They are people who sneak into our country. Let me list for you just a few documented crimes by illegals.

June 2006 an illegal rapes and kills two young Texas girls. He was caught, he did get the death penalty, however, we you and I fed this man in our prison system for two long years. Think about that for a minute. If a killer, rapist gets the death penalty why do we wait two years? I will never understand that.

May 2007 an illegal rapes and kills a young girl and runs back to his home country in Mexico. This man has never been caught. There are dozens of the same kind of story.

July 2008 an illegal kills a man and his two grown sons during a road rage situation. This happened in San Francisco you must know San Francisco is a sanctuary city. This means that if a man is stopped for as little as a driving infraction his illegality can not be reported to the authorities. Arrest and release is the practice. No one can be questioned or reported to ICE. Our government hands over millions of dollars to these cities. I believe the United States should cut funding to any and all sanctuary cities in our country.

The police have their hands tied in these cities. It seems to me these cities take better care of the illegals than they do their own citizens. What are we thinking to allow illegals to come here and mess up our country.

Yes, I believe in the death penalty. If any person rapes and kills a child in this country weather he is illegal or not that person should be put to death. We waste millions of dollars keeping these people incarcerated while we have babies going to bed at night hungry.

In my view an illegal should not have one given right in this country. I have heard it said that theses people, illegals, will do work most Americans will not. That could be true, but what does that say about us Americans. Why are we Americans hiring illegals?

Remember I talked about the speaker of the house Nancy Pelosi? She owns hotels and a lot of real-estate in California. I read in 2007 that an investigation was to happen just to look into her hires. I waited and watched to see what would happen and I was not surprised that nothing happened. I would bet the farm if there really was an investigation we would learn the truth. Once again the secular progressives are winning.

Why did 9/11 happen? The worse event in the history of our country. It happened because there are country's and people who hate us. Illegals are all around us, in our schools, neighborhoods, and even in our churches. Are they all bad? No they are not but the good ones should step up and be counted.

All the negatives about Muslims. Are they all bad? I do not think so, I believe the very moderate ones are good people. But have we ever even once seen one of them denounce the violence and hatred of their people?

Domestic terrorism is on the rise in this country. Even some of our own have turned, they are torching churches, hurting innocent people and creating chaos. So many bad things, such as fire bombs placed in police cars and attacking families in their homes. Our world is filled with concern but also with hypocrisy. The hypocrisy is on the part of the people who "see no evil, speak no evil" all because they do not want to get involved. You need to declare what side you are on. Are you a traditional conservative or a secular progressive?

I recently read a book called <u>Islam in America</u> written by a friend of mine author Marshall Frank. If you are interested in knowing the truth and the real acts about Islamic Muslims please read this book. You will be stunned!

An illegal can ask for and receive a court appointed attorney. We are paying that tab. Illegals can go to the emergency room, get care and we are paying the tab. Remember General Ramsey Clark? He defended Saddam Hussein. What was he thinking? Most democrats are against the death penalty, mandatory sentencing, and the three-strike law. They are however, for programs the very programs we pay for. This gives me pause because how are our police supposed to do their jobs. We need to put a stop to political correctness in this country and let the police do their jobs. If we allow this influx of illegals to continue, I promise you they will ruin this country.

There are a handful of government official's who are willing to tackle this problem, we need to once again become proactive. We should be outraged all over this country. Trust me, if a job is available it should be given to an American. For those lazy taking from the government. Track them down and make them work. Get those people off food stamps and welfare checks. I believe if our government did a better job our welfare system would be a good thing for those who really need help. But as it is now the corruption in the welfare system is on overload.

Most of the stories about illegals are buried inside the paper. No one wants you to know how rampant the crime really is. Tom Trankito is all over this issue. He seems to be the only voice I hear. Hopefully his influence in the Senate will help

March 2007 an illegal was shot by a boarder patrol officer while doing drug running into the United States. Guess who goes to jail? You guessed it, the boarder patrol officer. I say shoot to kill! What is wrong with our system? Since when does an illegal drug runner get to get on the stand and discuss his circumstances against our own people? This story has more to it but frankly, I do not care as a n American how and why.

We want immigrants here, this is what has made this country great. Our parents and grandparents made America what it is today. But the difference is they came legally.

English is and should always be the first language. 55 years ago when I was in school it was mandatory that we learn Spanish. Two years of Spanish or you did not graduate. I went to school in Florida I always thought this mandatory class was because we lived but a stones throw away from Cuba. But I can also tell you the Cubans who came to our shores to be educated had to know English.

We need every citizen of the United States to learn English, no matter where you are from. I do not know how you feel, but it really upsets me to call my local phone company and be asked to press one for English. How does a foreign speaking person even get phone service? If I chose to move to France, I would learn French. Even when I visited France and Italy I made sure I at least knew the basics. I had no trouble with the language barrier. Some foreigners that come here know not one word of English.

August 8, 2008 Newsflash today

Because ICE can not find the majority of illegals, they have suggested "illegals leave the country on their own instead of risking being caught and charged." I was shocked. Like that will ever happen. Our government can not even find these people! Until one commits a crime they can not be found. God help us. My questions are, check the hospitals, schools, colleges and work places. I bet a good volunteer team in these cities could track some of the illegals. Especially the boarder cities.

Parents be aware they are all around us. Find out in your town where the pedifiles are. The next story will open your eyes. How do we protect our children with this kind of governing? Our system is broken!

Mexican troops cross border, hold border agent:

This story was a News Max August 6, 2008

Mexican troops crossed the border into Arizona and held a U.S. Border Patrol agent at gunpoint on Sunday, according to a published report. Agents assigned to the Border Patrol at Ajo, Arizona said the Mexican soldiers crossed the border into an isolated area southwest of Tucson and pointed rifles at the agent, who has not been identified. The Mexicans withdrew after other American agents arrived on the scene, The Washington Times reports. It is not known why the troops crossed the border, but American law enforcement authorities have said the current and former Mexican soldiers have been hired to protect drug and immigrant smugglers. "Unfortunately, this sort of behavior by Mexican military personnel has been going on for years." Union local 2544 of the National Border Patrol Council said on its web site.

"They are never held accountable, and the United States government will undoubtedly brush this off as another case of misunderstanding. Oh well, they didn't know they were in the United States. It is fortunate that this incident didn't end in a very ugly gunfight." Ricardo Alday, a spokesman at the Mexican Embassy in Washington, told the Times on Tuesday: "Law enforcement operations have led, from time to time, to innocent incursions by both U.S. and Mexican law enforcement personnel and military units into the territory of both nations...

"We always try to solve these incidents in a cooperative fashion, and as acknowledged by the Border Patrol, this was the case in the episode at Ajo." The General Accounting Office estimates that $23 billion in illegal drugs flow across the border each year

According to The Times, a coalition of border sheriffs has demanded that the American and Mexican governments probe incursions into the U.S. by heavily armed drug escorts dressed in Mexican military uniforms.

Who is to blame? Our government.

Chapter Thirteen
What Can Be Done?

Well I hope you have enjoyed this book. But mostly I hope your eyes have been opened. I hope you are opened enough to recognize yourself as the parent that is responsible for the bad behavior of your child. I am hoping you are enraged. I am hoping that you become aware that even the slightest action on your part as the parent can and will influence your child. When you make a mistake, let your child know you did.

Many parents must both work outside of the home today. I understand that life style however, who and how is your child being raised? Do you have competent people teaching and handling your role as a parent correctly? Be selective.

Some parents believe giving their child everything is the answer. I think you know in your hearts that it is not the answer. A child learns early on how to get what they want.

Let us travel through the chapters in this book and discern together what we as concerned parents, Americans, and God fearing parents should be doing.

Chapter one

Watch closely what your kids are allowed to watch on TV. What CDs are you allowing them to listen to. You are the parent you are the person paying for their entertainment. Do not trust your child. Check their activities on the computer. Keep your computer where you can visually see it. You child should have the fear of being caught not you having the fear of catching them. Let them earn your trust.

Chapter Two

Learn about your local judges. Just voting is not the answer. Research the laws, if you are not happy about them, your vote will be even more important. Believe me, with a little effort you can change things. Never believe one voice cannot make a difference.

Chapter Three

Do you belong to a church or a synagogue? Teaching your child about religion starts very young. Do you say prayers at meals and at bedtime? Do you have religious values to pass on? How about prayers for sick family members or friends? Start today if you have not been doing this before. How do you treat your elderly parents and friends? Remember your child is watching you. Without God in your lives nothing else matters.

Chapter Four

Nothing in your professional life is worth anything if you have failed to raise a child correctly. No wealth or stature means a hoot without your child becoming a decent human being. All you live and speak becomes part and parcel of your child. Remember you and you alone are the major teacher in your child's life.

Chapter Five

The media is biased. The media has become corrupt. Just because your local paper indorses a candidate does not mean they have it right. All the junk you see on TV and read in the newspaper should not influence your thought process. What should happen is your curiosity about truth should prevail. Check out the reports you see and hear. Filter out the junk and make good decisions. Do your homework.

Chapter Six

Exercise your mind. Again do not believe what you hear and read. Become proactive and investigate. The politicians today, are dishonest. Keep in mind not all of them are dishonest, but unfortunately, most are. Lets hold them accountable. Lets never again accept their lies and misspoken junk. One vote at a time is all it takes. Use that vote to clean up our cities, states and our great country. Forget partisan politics forget that you are a democrat or a republican. Watch the pork spending in Washington, that alone will tell you what kind of governor, senator or congressmen you voted into office. No matter what we do, how knowledgeable we are, we can and will make mistakes. Do that for your kids. They are our future.

Chapter Seven

We are all God creature. How could any person believe God would want one race to be more inferior to the other? Enough is enough about the 100 year old slavery stories. Blacks and whites need to work much harder than they have in the past to get beyond the blame and hate game. Remember we are all Americans. God loves us all equally.

Chapter Eight

Respect to me is a very easy concept. Everyday our friends and family show respect to one another by unseen ways and attitudes. Respect is up there with loving and caring for one another. Thank you, please and your welcome are just words we learn as children. Words and actions together are what respect is all about. Parents do a better job! Kudos to those of you who are doing it right. Teaching never ends in your life in regards to your kids. I find myself from time to time correcting my adult kids when I notice them faltering in the respect department. And I also know we all falter. Some days it is hard to put the happy face on and do everything right. We are human beings after all.

Chapter Nine

Patriotism, what a wonderful word. What a beautiful and wonderful country we are blessed to live in. Is it perfect? No, but it is ours. I love my country and I hope all of you do too. Our military is awesome. We should praise them everyday and we should pray for them every day. To be an American is the ultimate. We can pray or not. We can vote or not. We can pursue our own lifestyle, we can fly our flag with pride, we can dispute our very own government. That is freedom. Some countries hate us. We can not stop their hatred but we can stop it here, little by little we can chip away the hatred in our towns, cities and states. When I see celebrities and others go to foreign countries and knock America, it sickens me. How dare they. Teach your child to be patriotic. Place your hand over your heart when you say the Pledge of Allegiance. American allows ordinary people to become extraordinary. Fly that beautiful flag with pride, tell your kids how proud you are. They will follow you, I promise. When I see a small child waving a flag at a parade I always wonder if their parents have explained the meaning of waving the flag.

Chapter Ten

I cannot stress enough what I see everyday. I could fill 100 pages with disturbing actions I see with our youths today. I think you have the picture when you look in the eyes of your child, what do you see? Love is what you see. Trust is what you see. Those kids need you to teach them how to show love and trust, they are hungry to learn respect and discipline. Remember how hard it was to potty train that child? Think about how long it takes to help them learn to walk and read. Your job after those tasks has just begun. Put all your efforts into teaching them proper behavior. I am so thrilled when my sons friends and associates rush up to me to greet me. Some of them kiss me some just offer their hands. The respect is wonderful however, some have neglected to teach their children to do the same thing. Why is that?

Chapter Eleven

I know I have offended some of you, maybe your child really needs the drugs they are taking or maybe not. Get other opinions, isn't your child worth it? Demand research on long term effects. As of this date we know too little. Knowledge is power, remember that.

Chapter Twelve

We simply need to stay on top of this problem. We need legislatures to stop the partisan politics and act. We can make lots of noise to our governors, senators, and even our President.

I hope you have learned something form this book. Many people my age have cheered me on because they too feel sad about our society and the decline in morals and values. Some of the grandparents I have spoken to are so disappointed in their own sons and daughters because of the manner in which they are raising their kids.

Believe me folks the decline is universal. We must change the direction in which this country is going. Only you can make those changes. Start today, do the best you can, no one can ask for more.

Remember evil does exist. Let us rid our lives from evil. It is a hard job, but it can be done one day at a time!

Epilogue

History was made today in the USA

The date is November 4, 2008. Election day. The American people have voted and we have a new president.. Today is the beginning of change in our country. We will not know what those changes will be for a long time. We will learn who our new leader will be and who he really is.

The disappointment I felt was overwhelming most of all because we as Americans do not know this man, however, I will respect this man and hope his promise of change happens.

I believe now the seculars in this country will lead us into socialism, I pray I am wrong.

I have listed some of the important issues to watch.

Religious rights

Our pocketbooks

National security

The fairness doctrine

Illegal immigration

Small business

The patriot act

Rulings by judges

And by far one of the most important, our great military.

I feel comfortable in my life now, because I am in the winter of my life- my worries are for our children. Will they live in a better and safer America?

The liberal judges are humming a happy tune today. The illegals are tickled pink. The people in Kenya are dancing in the streets.

Now) with a controlled Congress. Will we see fair and good? Maybe we will see the demise of our great consitution from the inside out.

Can I be wrong? Yes I can and I want to be wrong, my hope is that all of you will be aware of all the government is doing ant) will be doing,.

I will let go of my fears today, and I will support my new president, and the new administraticø I hope you will do the same. Never knock your president. The last few years of the George W, Bush hatred has been awful. We need to be better than that. No more hatred.

Sit back and acknowledge the change that is coming. Let's end the divide in America.

I will pray for the healing, and peace we all need, I will also pray for our new president, and hope for his wisdom to do all the right things. We need to prove to the world that we are patriotic Americans. And that we will step up to the plate and be all that we can be.

God bless America!

P I wont be quiet if I see bad things happening. My next book will be a diary of our new president as he begins his first years as our new leader of tile free world. I will be your watchdog,

Love, Gloria

Endnotes

Bill O'Reilly Page 5, 9, 33

John Gibson Page 19

Thomas Sowal Page 57

Marshall Frank Page 83

News Max Page 86

Gail Cross Page 31

Erosion

Webster's dictionary says "the wearing away of the earths surface by the actions of winds, glaciers etc. The state of being eroded."

Made in the USA
Las Vegas, NV
05 May 2022

48453945R00069